The Work of Lawlessness Revealed

By Donald Peart

The Work of Lawlessness Revealed Copyright © 2012 Donald A. Peart

All rights reserved. No part of this book may be reproduced in any form, except for noncommercial use in the inclusion of brief quotations in a review, without permission in writing from the author.

The King James is the Bible translation used for clarity relative to modern English, unless otherwise noted.

All bold text and literal parenthetical phrases in the Scripture references are added by the author for clarity

Dictionary reference, includes, but not limited to, Strong's Concordance, BibleWorks Software, and ISA2 Basic Software

ISBN: 978-0-9852481-3-0

Acknowledgments

In sincere appreciation, I credit the Holy Spirit and all the men of God and women of God who impacted to my life in Christ for the past 36 years.

Table of Contents

Introduction 1
Lawlessness Defined 3
The Work of Lawlessness 5
The Mystery of Lawlessness 7
The Mystery Man of Sin 9
Lawlessness in God's Temple 11
The Man of Sin Revealed 17
The Son of Perdition Revealed 20
The Lawless One Revealed 26
The Lawless Energy of Satan 31
The Cause of the Energy of Error 35
The Lie Defined 40
The Work of Lawlessness Defined 48
Signs of Demons 54
Jesus' Covenant — the Remedy for Lawlessness 60
Other Books

Introduction

On May 17, 2011, at approximately 3:40AM the Lord woke me up and spoke some things to me from Jeremiah 36 concerning writing. The Spirit of the Lord instructed me to write a scroll **again.** His instructed me to author this book which was completed on June 9, 2011.

This is what the Lord indicated to me. Since I am sometimes restrained, held back, confined from going to certain houses of God to speak His words like the words outlined in this book, He asked me to write His instructions so that ("the Baruchs" – Jeremiah 36) may read this book and declare it in places I am not able to go. I am also to write this book that others may read and hear unto obedience unto holiness.

Another purpose of this book is to encourage repentance which leads to forgiveness of sin and release from lawless works. The Lord said, "Take a scroll of a book and write on it all the words that I have spoken to you against Israel, against Judah, and against all the nations …. It may be that the house of Judah (the Church) will hear … that everyone may turn … that I may forgive their iniquity and their sin" **(Jeremiah 36:2-3).**

This book is for the day of fasting (the Day of Atonement[1]) and for all of Judah (worshippers of the living God) to read in their cities (Churches) – see **Jeremiah 36:6.** It may be as "the man of sin" is revealed (uncovered) in this book, some may present their supplication to the Lord turning from their work of lawlessness.

Those who read this book or teach the principles in this book to the Church of Jesus and teach the principles of this book to the

---

1 As the Feast of Passover is fulfilled in Jesus "Christ our Passover sacrifice for us;" and we are keeping this feast with "the unleavened [bread] of sincerity and truth;" and has the Feast of Pentecost is fulfilled in the giving of the Holy Spirit; so the Day of Atonement is a season of reflecting by humbling our souls, a season in which we will also get answers that lead us to repentance and forgiveness as God has atoned for our sins through Jesus, once.

nations will be as Baruch [("blessed") **Jeremiah 36:11-12]**. Yet, some may disregard this book, casting it out as contrary to their beliefs. Some may even put a knife to a book like this and may even burn the words of this book **(Jeremiah 36:23).**

However, the Lord has already commissioned apostles and prophets to write words like these; and they will yet write again **(Jeremiah 36:28).** May the Lord give repentance that leads to release of sins to all who seek Him! May the words of this book be a blessing to you!

Lawlessness Defined

1 John 3:4: Whoever commits sin also commits lawlessness, and sin is lawlessness.

There is a difference between the "work of lawlessness" and "lawlessness." In this section, I will be defining lawlessness. We see above that "sin is lawlessness." "Sin" is literally defined as "un-mark" (not sectioned out). "Sin" is also defined as missing the mark so as not to partake of the prize or allotment.

"Lawlessness" is defined as "illegality," "without law," or that which is "not parceled out," or that which is "not (the) norm." The Greek word "anomia" (lawlessness) is a compound of "a" (negation, not) and "nomos" ("norm," "law," "parceled out portion").

Thus, lawlessness is that which is "not parceled out" for use. Thus, if that which is not parceled out for use is used, then the use of something slated not to be use is lawlessness (think of Mr. and Mrs. Adam who ate from the tree that was not parceled out to them for use). Lawlessness is also that which is not considered as "normal" behavior. Social studies call this kind of behavior "deviant behavior" — behavior that is against "the norm."

Lawlessness is also "sin," which means that lawlessness can cause a person to forfeit their "prize," or intended "allotment" from God. There is also a contextual definition of lawlessness. Jesus defined lawlessness as "all uncleanness."

*Matthew 23:27-28: [27]Woe to you, scribes and Pharisees, hypocrites! For you are like whitewashed tombs which indeed appear beautiful outwardly, but **inside** are **full of dead men's bones and all uncleanness.** [28]Even so you also outwardly appear righteous to men, but inside you **are full of hypocrisy and lawlessness.***

We see in the reference above that Jesus **"liken"** "hypocrisy" to "dead men's bones." Jesus said that the Pharisees were **"like** whitewash tombs;" and that like these "tombs," the Pharisees appeared beautiful outwardly, but inwardly they were like "dead men's bones." Jesus said that the appearance of looking beautiful on the outside, and yet the inside being as "dead men's bones" is **"likened"** to "hypocrisy."

In other words, a hypocrite is a person that appears one way on the outside, but their internal thinking is opposite what he/she portrays. In the same element of thought Jesus also equated **"all uncleanness" to "lawlessness."** Note: Jesus did not say that "uncleanness" in general is "lawlessness." But that **"all uncleanness"** is lawlessness.

In other words, lawlessness encompasses "all" the acts of uncleanness been done in one's life at the same time. This makes a little more sense as can been seen in Paul's writing. Paul linked "all uncleanness" to "greediness" (lit., "covetousness," "more-having," "holding more" or "desiring) more."

*Ephesians 4:19: Who, being past feeling, have given themselves over to lewdness, to work **all uncleanness** with (lit., in) greediness.*

As we can see, the "act" of "all uncleanness" is "in greediness;" or the "act [of] all uncleanness" is "in desiring more." Thus, a lack of contentment is linked to all uncleanness; and "all uncleanness" is "like" lawlessness. Therefore, lawlessness may stem from a lack of contentment.

So "sin is lawlessness." "All uncleanness"[2] is "lawlessness." Lawlessness is that which is "not parceled out" for use. Lawlessness is also that which is not considered as "normal." Lawlessness is that which is "illegal." These definitions of lawlessness are important to know; because they are related to the "work of lawlessness."

---

[2] Judas' betrayal of Jesus was considered unclean (John 13), idol worship also causes uncleanness in spirit and flesh (2 Corinthians 6:14-18 and 2 Corinthians 7:1), etc.

The Work of Lawlessness

Matthew 7:23: And then I will declare to them, 'I never knew you; depart from Me, you who **practice lawlessness (lit., work lawlessness)***!'*

Jesus was the first to identify some as those who "'work' lawlessness." Jesus made this statement when He defined who could enter into the kingdom of heaven "in that day." Those who worked lawlessness could not enter into the kingdom of heaven.

Thus, the work of lawlessness has serious implications. What made Jesus' statement even more interesting is that the people whom He classed as "workers of lawlessness" claimed that they had cast out demons "to/with" His name and did many works of power "to/with" His name.

Matthew 7:22: [22]*Many will say to Me in that day, 'Lord, Lord, have we not* **prophesied in Your name, cast out demons in Your name, and done many wonders in Your name***?'* [23] *And then I will declare to them, 'I never knew you; depart from Me, you who* **practice lawlessness!***'*

Their statement of claim as to why they should enter the kingdom of heaven, based on works done "to" Jesus' name was refuted by Jesus. Jesus said that these same people "worked lawlessness." Thus, one must consider, "how" were the workers of lawlessness casting out demons? By "whom" were they prophesying? Why were they deceived to believe that they were "doing (or making) much power to [His] name?" What is this work of lawlessness that they were "doing" that disqualified them? This is a serious matter. Humans can claim that they are prophesying "to" and "with" Jesus name, and yet be disqualified to enter the kingdom of heaven. With that said, let us look at some key words in the text just cited.

First let us clarify the use of the word **"in"** in Matthew 7:22 of the New King James Version. The word translated as "in" in Matthew 7:22 is the Greek word "τῷ" **(the)** and not "ἐν" **(in)**; and the word ("τῷ") is "dative case." A word that is used in the "dative case" means that the word is "instrumental" (with) and "locative" (to). Here are some simple examples.

The boy gave the crown **to** the king. The boy was sealed **with** the king's ring. If this is understood, Matthew 7:22 could have been translated as such: "Many will say to Me in that day, 'Lord, Lord, have we not prophesied **'to [and] with'** Your name, cast out demons **'to [and] with'** Your name, and done many wonders **'to [and] with'** Your name?'"

So, there will be many who have prophesied "to" and "with" the name of Jesus, and yet they are "workers of lawlessness." There will be many who will cast out demons "to" and "with" the name of Jesus, and yet they are "workers of lawlessness." Thirdly, there will be many who have done or made many miracles or powers "to" and "with" the name of Jesus, and yet they are "workers of lawlessness."

Again, the question is: if many can demonstrate prophesy, cast out demons, and produce power, and yet be disqualified, with **what character** are they really doing these things?

With that said, in light of what was just discussed, I must also emphasize that there are indeed true prophecies that can be uttered in Jesus' name! Demons can truly be cast out in Jesus' name; and powers (miraculous powers) can indeed be done in Jesus name? Yet how do we explain Jesus' conclusion? How do we know what the work of lawlessness is in order that we do not partake of such lawlessness? The work of lawlessness is a mystery that the Spirit of Jesus has to reveal to us!

The Mystery of Lawlessness

*2 Thessalonians 2:7: For the **mystery of lawlessness is already at work (lit., in-work)**; only He who now restrains will do so until He is taken out of the way.*

The verse above is another place in the Bible where "lawlessness" is coupled with "work." Paul indicated that "the mystery of **lawlessness** is already '**in-working**'." Thus, Paul also discussed the "in-work" of lawlessness in some detail. Let us take a look at this mystery of the "in-working of lawlessness."

According to Paul, the mystery of lawlessness is called "the man of sin." The mystery of lawlessness is also called the "son of perdition." The mystery of lawlessness is a "he" that will be "showing himself that he is god."

2 Thessalonians 2:3-4; 7, KJV: ³*Let no man deceive you by any means: for [that day shall not come,] except there comes a falling away first, and that **man of sin** be revealed, the **son of perdition;** ⁴... **he as God sits in the temple of God, shewing himself that he is God** ... ⁷**For the mystery of iniquity (lit., lawlessness) doth already work....***

Next, we must also understand that the mystery of lawlessness can only be recognized when he is "revealed" after "he 'births himself' out of the middle." The mystery of lawlessness is linked to the "energy of error" which is the "energy of Satan." The mystery of lawlessness is linked to "the energy of Satan in all power … of falsehood, "signs … of falsehood" and "wonders of falsehood." The mystery of lawlessness is also linked to "the lie (or the falsehood)."

2 Thessalonians 2:7-11, KJV : ⁷***For the mystery of iniquity doth already work:** only he who now let (lit., restrains) will let (lit., restrain), **until he be taken out of the way (lit., unit he births himself out of the middle).** ⁸ And **then shall that Wicked be revealed** ... ⁹[Even him,] whose coming is after the **working (lit., energy) of Satan with all power and signs and lying wonders.** ¹⁰And ... because they received not the love of the truth, that they might* *be saved.* [11]*... God shall send them* **strong delusion (lit., energy of error),** *that they should believe* **a lie (lit., the falsehood).**

The verses cited in this chapter are "hard to be understood" for some, as Peter himself said of Paul's writing ***(2 Peter 3:16).*** Thus, I will write brief sections (chapters) concerning each of the items in 2 Thessalonians 2:1-11 that Paul associated to the "in-work of lawlessness," and then show how they link to Jesus' statement concerning those who "work lawlessness."

The Mystery Man of Sin

*2 Thessalonians 2:3: … For that Day will not come unless the falling away comes first, and the **man of sin** is revealed, the son of perdition.*

The work of lawlessness or the "in-working of the lawlessness" is "the man of sin." Some claim the man of sin will be only "a man" (the beast king of Revelation 13 and Revelation 17). This interpretation is true, but there is more to truth of the man of sin.[3]

However, following the pattern of Paul's writing, "the man of sin" is an inclusive name Paul used to identify the **"old man" (the old nature)** that was "in" us before we became Jesus' disciples. Paul called the **"old man** … that **body of sin."** In other words, the **"man** of sin" is also "the old **man"** which is also called "the body of **sin."** The old man, the man of sin, is the sinful nature in all mankind, especially those without Jesus in their lives.

*Romans 6:6: Knowing this, that our **old man** was crucified with Him, that the **body of sin** might be done away with, that we should no longer be **slaves of sin.***

We see here that the "old man" is the "body of sin." Thus, this "body of sin" is **"'the old man' of sin!"** The "old man" is another name for the "man of sin." "The man of sin" in mankind (as a "body" of people) is a picture of those who are "slaves of sin." For Christians, sin is supposed to be our "former conduct" before God created us into a "new man" in Christ.

Ephesians 4:22; 24: [22]*That you **put off**, concerning your **former conduct, the old man** which grows corrupt according to the deceitful lusts …* [24]*and that you **put on the new man** which was created according to God, in true righteousness and holiness.*

In the text above, Paul calls the "old man" our "former conduct" (**"former** conduct" for those who are born from above out of

---

[3] You may reference my books, *the beast,* and *The False Prophet, Alias, Another Beast*

God). So, the "old man" is a way of defining our "former conduct;" it follows that the "man of sin" is a way of defining the **"former"** corrupt way we "conducted" ourselves as former sinners. We must now "put on the **new man**!"

*Colossians 3:9-10: ⁹Do not lie to one another, since you have put off the **old man** with his deeds, ¹⁰and have put on the **new man** who is renewed in knowledge according to the image of Him who created him.*

The man of sin is the old man, or our old manner of life. "The new man" is the "man according to the image" of God. The new man is our new manner of life. The new man is the "man …in … righteousness." The new man is the "man … in … holiness (lit., intrinsically right)." The new man has God's knowledge and God's image.

Thus, we have seen that the new man points to our new lifestyle through salvation. "The man of sin" points to our **"old"** sinful conduct. However, the redeemed must "put on the new man" through faith in Jesus Christ!

Lawlessness in God's Temple

2 Thessalonians 2:3-8: *³Let no one deceive you by any means; for that Day will not come unless the falling away comes first, and the man of sin is revealed, the son of perdition, ⁴who opposes and exalts himself above all that is called God or that is worshiped, so that he sits as God **in the temple of God,** showing himself that he is God.*

The mystery of lawlessness will be doing its lawless work in the temple of God. In God's temple, the man of sin, the son of perdition will act like he is God; and demonstrate that he is a god. The other mystery is: what (who) is the mystery of the "temple of God, as it relates to the man of sin?"

Is the temple of God a future manmade temple in Jerusalem? No! The Jews may indeed build a temple again in Jerusalem because some evangelicals are falsely pushing this narrative.[4] However, the temple was destroyed in AD70 by Titus, as prophesied by Jesus, to bring an end to animal sacrifices. Why? Jesus' sacrifice is meant to end all animal sacrifices forever **(Hebrews 10:18, Romans 10:4, Daniel 9:27).**

According to Jesus, another cause for the destruction of the temple is because most of the Jews rejected Jesus and most are still rejecting Jesus **(Luke 19:41-44; 21:20-21; Matthew 23:37-24:2).** Our Lord Jesus said that Jerusalem is **not** the "place" of worship **(John 4:20-21).** In the Spirit is now the place of worship **(John 4:23-24; Philippians 3:3).**

I must also note that any Christian that reinstitute animal sacrifices as an instrument of atonement "has trampled the Son of God underfoot, counted the blood of the covenant by which he was sanctified a common thing, and insulted the Spirit of grace" **(Hebrews 10:29).**

---

4 God no longer dwell in temples made with hands. The Israelites, themselves, are to become the temple of God through Jesus Christ.

Is the temple of God a manmade temple where the Church has to meet? No! Some in the Church world have now made "their" manmade Church building "the" temple of God. Stephen in Acts 7:47-48 said "But Solomon built Him a house. However, **the Most High does not dwell in temples made with hands**, as the prophet says." The apostle Paul said something similar to Stephen in Acts 17:2, "God, who made the world and everything in it, since He is Lord of heaven and earth, **does not dwell in temples made with hands."**

God considers manmade temples and manmade tabernacles as "worldly." The tabernacle built by Moses is considered a "worldly sanctuary." "Then verily the first covenant had also ordinances of divine service, and a **worldly** sanctuary... But Christ being come a high priest of good things to come, by a greater and **more perfect (lit., mature)** tabernacle, **not made with hands,** that is to say, not of this building (lit., creation)."[5] Now that Jesus has come, any emphasis on temples made with hands is considered "immature" and outdated. Temples made with hands are also considered "worldly."

The emphasis on building manmade Church edifices have supplanted the truth of building believers (the true temple of God). Some have even gone as far as to make the pulpit area the altar. The altar of God is not some manmade raised platform with these high-back chairs for the elders and pastors to sit.

Jesus is our Altar of Incense! That is, Jesus is our intercessor. Jesus is our Brazen Altar! That is, Jesus is our place of sacrifice *(Hebrews 13:10).* **The New Testament** says that **"the Lord God Almighty and the Lamb is the temple"** of New Jerusalem who mothered us *(Revelation 21:22; Galatians 4:24).* **The New Testament** says that the **Church** is the "building fitly framed together that grows into a **holy temple** in the Lord" *(Ephesians 2:21).*

---

5 Hebrews 9:1; 9:11

Here is another question, is our bodies the temple of God? Yes! God no longer live in temple made with hands. The Church is the temple of God. So, here is another intriguing question, how can the man of sin work in God's temple or what is the mystery of "the work of lawlessness" in "the temple of God?"

1 Corinthians 6:13b: ... *Now **the body [is]** ... **for the Lord** ....*

1 Corinthians 6:19: *Or do you not know that **your body is the temple of the Holy Spirit** [who] is in you....*

1 Corinthians 3:16: ***Do you not know that you are the temple of God*** *....*

1 Corinthians 3:17: ***If anyone defiles the temple of God,*** *God will destroy him.* ***For the temple of God is holy, which [temple] you are.***

Every human body was created to be the temple of the Lord God. The unsaved is just not aware of how valuable their bodies are! We just read that "the **body** is ... **for** the Lord." We also read that "**your body** is the **temple** of the Holy Spirit." Paul also said that "you are the temple of God." **Thus, the temple of God is our bodies.**

Whether we are saved or unsaved (a Christian or a non-Christian), "the body" was made to be "the temple of God." Now, "whomever" we allow to live in the temple of our bodies is relative. When we become a disciple of Jesus our bodies become God's temple; and God will come and live in us (His temple) by the Holy Spirit.

However, whoever does not serve Jesus, and does not allow the Spirit of Jesus to inhabit them (sit as King, Lord, Priest, Apostle, etc.) in the temple of their bodies; another entity like the man of sin, another entity like Satan, another entity like lawlessness will eventually sit in the temple of those bodies (the temple originally made for God) acting like a god. This indeed is a "mystery!"

The body (the temple of God) can be occupied by the man of sin. The man of sin can show itself to be god in God's temple for those who do not allow Jesus to abolish the work of lawlessness in their lives. And this "mystery of lawlessness" is that the sin nature acts like god in the body of sin of those deceived by its "power." The Bible said that "sin" has a "power;" and that sin's power is "the law" — "the law of sin."

1 Corinthians 15:56: ... *The **strength (lit., power)** of sin is **the law.***

Romans 7:23: *But I see **another law** in my members, warring against the law of my mind, and bringing me into captivity to the **law of sin** which is in my members.*

We just saw that the "power of sin" is "the law" which give rise to "another law," the "law of sin," or lawlessness (for **1 John 3** says sin is lawlessness). The "law of sin" is "legalism." 'Legalism" can be defined as humans and spirits using the "spiritual law" as "a starting point," a "base of operation" for condemnation by highlighting sin that produces more sinfulness!

Romans 7:8a: *But sin, **taking opportunity** by the commandment, **produced** in me all [manner of evil] desire*

Romans 7:14: *For we know that the **law is spiritual**, but I am carnal, sold under sin.*

The Law is "spiritual." The Law needs the "Spirit of Life" (love and mercy) of Jesus Christ in order for God's law to be fulfilled in us in a positive way **(Romans 8:1-4).** However, according to Paul "sin" can become so strong through legalism (the law of sin) that sin will cause the sinful nature (the man of sin) to become a "controller" in the temple of God. This power of the law of sin can so deceive us that our bodies (the temple of God) can begin to do things we do not "will (choose) to do." Paul discussed this in detail in Romans 7. He calls it "another law" (the law of sin) warring against the law of his mind.

Romans 7:15-25: [15]*For what I am doing, I do not understand. **For what I will to do, that I do not practice;** but what I hate, that I do.* [16]*If,* *then, I do what I will not to do, I agree with the law that it is good.* **[17]But now, it is no longer I who do it, but sin that dwells in me ...** [20]*Now if I do what I will not to do, it is no longer I who do it, but **sin that dwells in me**.* [21]*I find then a law, that evil is present with me, the one who wills to do good.* [22]*For I delight in the law of God according to the inward man.* [23]*But I see another law in my members, warring against the law of my mind, and bringing me into captivity to the **law of sin** which is in my members.* [24] *O wretched man that I am! Who will deliver me from this body of death?* [25]*I thank God – through Jesus Christ our Lord! So then, with the mind I myself serve the law of God, but with the flesh the law of sin.*

Therefore, do not think it strange that the man of sin can sit in the temple of God showing himself to be god. It is just another way of saying that if we do not allow the blood of Jesus, the baptism by water into Jesus Christ, the Word of Jesus, the Spirit of Jesus Christ, etc. to put to death the sin nature in us; the temple of God (our human bodies) can be controlled by sin.

And this sinful nature will eventually be "energized" to work false signs, wonders and powers deceiving people to believe the lie. The Bible teaches that legalism (law) also manifest "power." So, we have to be careful not to overly religious in the temple of God.

*1 Corinthians 15:56: ... The **strength (lit., power)** of sin is **the law.***

*Romans 7:23: But I see another law in my members, warring against the law of my mind, and bringing me into captivity to the **law of sin** which is in my members.*

*Galatians 3:5: Therefore, He who supplies the Spirit to you and **works miracles (lit., works powers)** among you, does He do it by the **works of the law**, or by the **hearing of faith**?*

Paul said that the "power of sin is the law." Paul also hinted that "works of power" can be performed by two entities, "law" or "faith" in Galatians 3:5 cited above. Churches that are overly legalists do see acts of power sometimes.

However, I must ask the question: are these acts of power by "law (legalism)" or by "the hearing of faith?" Are these acts of power being done in the temple of God through lawlessness (the law of sin,)? The law of sin appears to also have a legalistic "power" with it.

Thus, let us make sure we walk in love and mercy that our temples may be used for its intended purpose. We are "the temple of God." Do not allow lawlessness or the "work of lawlessness" (a manifestation of the law of sin) to act like a god in our bodies by showing the wrong kind of power. "Knowing this, that **our old man was crucified with [Him] (Jesus),** that the **body of sin might be done away with,** that we should no longer be slaves of sin **(Romans 6:6).** Our "body is the temple of the Holy Spirit" **(1 Corinthians 6:19).**

The Man of Sin Revealed

*2 Thessalonians 2:3-8: ³Let no one deceive you by any means; for that Day will not come unless the falling away comes first, and the **man of sin is revealed,** the son of perdition, ⁴who opposes and exalts himself above all that is called God or that is worshiped, so that he sits as God in the temple of God, **showing** himself that he is God … ⁶… that **he may be revealed** in his own time. ⁷For the mystery of lawlessness is already at work … until he is taken out of the way. ⁸And **then the lawless one will be revealed ….***

Paul said that the day of Christ cannot come except "the man of sin is revealed." "The man of sin revealed" is "the lawless one …revealed." There is another truth here; the man of sin (the sinful nature) can only be known by "revelation."[6] It takes God to uncover sin as sin, in order to bring man to repentance (a change of the mind) from practicing sin.

The sin demon blinds. Contrarily, God wants to uncover sinfulness in order to heal us from sin. There are also other ways the man of sin is revealed (exposed).

The man of sin will be exposed as he "opposes and exalts himself above all that is called God or that is worshiped, so that he sits as god in the temple of God, **showing** himself that he is god … that **he may be revealed.**" The man of sin will be revealed when "he births himself out of the middle."

The man of sin, the old man is revealed (uncovered) whenever man's old sinful nature in opposition of God is manifested. Here is a simple example. We hear an inner voice of God telling us to serve God and attend Church related meetings; however, we hear another inner voice (the sinful nature) telling us not to worship God or not to attend Church related meetings. In the

---

6 Dr. Kelley Varner

simple example just stated, the man of sin opposed God and the sinful nature exalted himself against the worship of God.

The man of sin (the sin nature in mankind) is also revealed when the sinful nature become a god unto himself.[7] He sits as god in the temple of God (the human body) showing himself that he is a god. There are many who declare that they are gods *(Ezekiel 28:2).*[8] Some also believe that there is no Creator; and that they do not need God; or they do not need to believe in the living God.

The man of sin is also revealed when he "shows" himself that he is a god by pseudo (false) "all power," "signs" and "wonders." **"Showing"** is from the Greek word "apodeikumi." It is used four places in the Scriptures and translated in the New King James as "attested," "prove," "displayed," and "showing."

Acts 2:22: Men of Israel, hear these words: Jesus of Nazareth, a Man ***attested (or showing)*** *by God to you* ***by miracles, wonders, and signs*** *which God did through Him in your midst, as you yourselves also know.*

Acts 25:7: When he had come, the Jews who had come down from Jerusalem stood about and laid many serious complaints against Paul, which they could not ***prove.***

1 Corinthians 4:9: For I think that God has ***displayed*** *us, the apostles, last, as men condemned to death; for we have been made a spectacle to the world, both to angels and to men.*

2 Thessalonians 2:3-9, KJV: [3]*Let no man deceive you by any means: for [that day shall not come,] except there comes a falling away first, and that* ***man of sin be revealed*** *... so that he as God sits in the temple of God,* ***shewing (Greek: apodeikunimia)*** *himself that he is God ...And then shall that Wicked be revealed ... whose coming is after the working (lit., energy) of Satan* ***with all power and signs and lying wonders.***

---

7 See my book *The False Prophet, Alias, Another Beast*
8 For the students of the Bible, I am aware of John 10:34-35 in opposition to Ezekiel 28:2, etc.

There will come a time when the man of sin (the sinful nature) will be revealed (uncovered). This will happen whenever he sits in God's temple (the body) **"proving"** himself to be a god while the person is living in sin (believing and practicing things that are opposite God and His Word). He will show himself a god by powers of falsehood, signs of falsehood and wonders of falsehood through an unclean lifestyle.

Remember in Chapter 2—"The Work of Lawlessness," we discussed how Jesus said there would be "workers of lawlessness" who professed to do power acts, who profess to cast out of demons and claimed to prophesy in His name. Jesus gave the hint that false signs can flow from the work of lawlessness. These false signs look like the real signs. However, Jesus revealed the source of the mimicking signs to be works of lawlessness.

The "man of sin" the "old [sinful] human" nature in mankind will become so lawless that he will eventually mankind by mimicking Jesus by the "showing" of miracles, except the man of sin's miracles will be pseudo (false). Remember, the word "attested" in Acts 2:22 is the same Greek word for "showing" in 2 Thessalonians 2:4.

Jesus was **"shown" by God** to you by miracles, wonders, and signs." In like manner, the man of sin through the energy of Satan will be shown (revealed) by pseudo miracles to reinforce the belief of the lie of lawlessness over the truth. This will be a result of the "work of lawlessness" in full effect which will be defined in the final section of this book.

The Son of Perdition Revealed

2 Thessalonians 2:3: *Let no one deceive you by any means; for that Day will not come unless the falling away comes first, and the man of sin is **revealed, the son of perdition (or destruction).***

John 17:12: *While I was with them in the world, I kept them in Your name. Those whom You gave Me I have kept; and none of them is lost except the **son of perdition (or destruction)**, that the Scripture might be fulfilled.*

"The man of sin" is the "son of perdition." Jesus called Judas, the one who betrayed Jesus, "the son of perdition." Therefore, an understanding of the "man of sin" can also be gleaned from Judas, the son of perdition. Here are <u>some</u> truths about Judas that will also apply to those who chose to walk in the nature of the man of sin.

Judas ("the son of perdition") started as **an apostle chosen** by Jesus. The man of sin can point to followers of Jesus who are chosen by Jesus, yet they did not put to death the old man of sin, the old sinful nature; and thus, eventually lose their life and "office."

Luke 6:13-16: *[13]... He called His disciples to Himself; and from them He **chose** twelve whom He also **named apostles:** [14]Simon, whom He also named Peter, and Andrew ... James and John; Philip and ... [16] ... **Judas Iscariot** ....*

Acts 1:16-17; 20: *[16]"Men and brethren, this Scripture had to be fulfilled, which the Holy Spirit spoke before by the mouth of David concerning **Judas**, who **became** a guide to those who arrested Jesus; [17]"for he was numbered with us and obtained a part in this ministry"... [20]"For it is written in the book of Psalms: 'Let his dwelling place be desolate, And let no one live in it'; and, 'Let another take his **office.**'"*

Judas ("the son of perdition") **"became"** a traitor. Thus, if the man of sin, the old man is not put to death as Paul taught, that person may eventually **become** a betrayer to those who are of Christ. Another way of defining "becoming a traitor is: some will **become** "antichrists." Antichrists are those who used to follow Jesus and then became anti-Jesus and did not continue with His Church.

*Luke 6:16: … Judas Iscariot who also **became** a traitor.*

*1 John 2:18-19: ¹⁸Little children, it is the last hour; and as you have heard that the Antichrist is coming, even now **many antichrists** have come, by which we know that it is the last hour. ¹⁹ **They went out from us**, but they were not of us; **for if they had been of us, they would have continued with us;** but they went out that they might be made manifest, that none of them were of us.*

Judas ("the son of perdition") was at one point called a "sheep" among the "twelve" apostles which shows that he was at one point a "sheep" of Jesus.

*Matthew 10:5; 16: ⁵**These twelve** Jesus sent out and commanded them, saying: Do not go into the way of the Gentiles, and do not enter a city of the Samaritans … ¹⁶ Behold, I send you out **as sheep** in the midst of wolves. Therefore, be wise as serpents and harmless as doves.*

Judas ("the son of perdition") cast out demons, cleanses the leper, healed the sick, and raised the dead before he betrayed Jesus. Potential betrayers can also do acts of power, as Jesus pointed out in **Matthew 7:21-23**. The measure of salvation is not casting out demons, but that our names are written in heaven *(Luke 10:20)*.

*Matthew 10:2-8: ²Now the names of the twelve apostles are these: first, Simon, who is called Peter, … and **Judas Iscariot, who also betrayed Him**. ⁵**These twelve** Jesus sent out and commanded them, saying … ⁸**"Heal the sick, cleanse the lepers**, raise the dead, **cast out demons** …."*

*Matthew 7:22-23: ²²"Many will say to Me in that day, 'Lord, Lord, have we not prophesied in Your name, **cast out demons in Your name, and done many wonders in Your name?'** ²³"And then I will declare to* them, '**I never knew you;** depart from Me, you who **practice lawlessness!**'"

Jesus called Judas ("the son of perdition") a devil. There will be other devils in the last days.

John 6:70-71: [70]*Jesus answered them, "Did I not choose you, the twelve, and one of you is* **a devil?"** [71] *He spoke of* **Judas** *Iscariot, the son of Simon, for it was he who would betray Him, being one of the twelve.*

2 Timothy 3:1-3: [1]*But know this, that in the last days perilous times will come:* [2]*For* **men will be ... slanderers (lit., devils)....**

Judas ("the son of perdition") kept the "money-box" (lit., tongue of the world). Money is the language of the world—"money talks." Money in general and betrayal **"money"** is a "language" of the man of sin, the son of perdition **(Matthew 21:12-13).** The emphasis of collecting or making "wages of unrighteousness" may be a sign of falsehood **(2 Peter 2 and Jude 1).**

John 12:3-6: [3]*Then Mary took a pound of very costly oil of spikenard, anointed the feet of Jesus, and wiped His feet with her hair ...* [4]*Then ...* **Judas** *Iscariot, Simon's son, who would betray Him, said,* [5] *"Why was this fragrant oil not sold for three hundred denarii and given to the poor?"* [6] *This he said, not that he cared for the poor, but because he was* **a thief,** *and had the* **money box (Greek: language (of the) world);** *and he used to take what was put in it.*

Matthew 26:15: And said unto them, what will ye give me, and I will deliver him unto you? **And they covenanted with [Judas] for thirty pieces of silver.**

Judas ("the son of perdition") received money (the "language (of the) world") to betray Jesus. The man of sin nature in some will betray the truth and the true saints in order to be able to "buy and sell" in the beast system. The Pharisees bribed workers of the beast's system of their day to keep silent about Jesus' resurrection.

Mark 14:10-11: ¹⁰*Then **Judas** Iscariot, one of the twelve, went to the chief priests to betray Him to them.* ¹¹*And when they heard it, they were glad, **and promised to give him money**. So, he sought how.*

Matthew 28:12-15: ¹²*When they had assembled with the elders and consulted together, they gave a **large sum of money** to the soldiers,* ¹³*saying, "Tell them, 'His disciples came at night and stole Him away while we slept.'* ¹⁴ *"And if this comes to the governor's ears, we will appease him and make you secure."* ¹⁵ ***So they took the money and did as they were instructed**; and this saying is commonly reported among the Jews until this day.*

John 12:4-6: ⁴*…**Judas** Iscariot, Simon's son, who would betray Him …* ⁶*… was **a thief and** had the **money box (Greek: glossokomon (language (of the) world)**; and he used to take what was put in it.*

*Revelation 13:17: And that no one may **buy or sell** except one who has the mark or the name of the beast, or the number of his name.*

As Satan entered Judas ("the son of perdition") more than once, in like manner, the man of sin will be energized by Satan.

John 13:26-27: ²⁶ *Jesus answered, "It is he to whom I shall give a piece of bread when I have dipped it." And having dipped the bread, He gave it to **Judas** Iscariot, the son of Simon.* ²⁷*Now after the piece of bread, **Satan entered him**. Then Jesus said to him, "What you do, do quickly."*

2 Thessalonians 2:3-9, KJV: ³*… that **man of sin be revealed, the son of perdition**…whose coming is after **the working (lit., energy) of Satan** with all power and signs and lying wonders.*

Thus, "the man of sin," the "son of 'destruction'" also points to the Judas-like believers who will eventually betray some in the Church. The name of the beast, the mark (character) of the beast and the number of the beast will be accepted by the Judas-like people so that they can maintain their ability to buy and sell in the system of beast. The corporate man of sin will be falsely convinced that he is god or from God by the energy of Satan; and the man of sin will in turn persecute the true Church of Jesus.

John 16:2, KJV: They shall put you out of the synagogues: yes, **the time cometh, that whosoever kills you will think that he doeth God service.**

With all of the above said, I know some of you are asking, "How do a saint identify those who are like Judas?" We will be able to know who are Judas-like by leaning on the **bosom** of Jesus. In Jesus' bosom answers are declared.

John 13:23-26: ²³Now there was leaning on Jesus' **bosom** *one of His disciples, whom Jesus loved. ²⁴Simon Peter therefore motioned to him to ask who it was of whom He spoke. ²⁵Then, leaning back on Jesus' breast, he said to Him, "Lord, who is it?" ²⁶Jesus answered, "It is he to whom I shall give a piece of bread when I have dipped it." And having dipped the bread, He gave it to Judas Iscariot, the son of Simon.*

We can know those who are Judas-like through others who dwell in the bosom of Jesus. Peter asked John to ask Jesus to tell him who the betrayer was.

John 13:23-26: ²³Now there was leaning on Jesus' bosom one of **His disciples, whom Jesus loved. ²⁴Simon Peter therefore motioned to him to ask who it was of whom He spoke.** *²⁵ Then, leaning back on Jesus' breast, he said to Him, "Lord, who is it?" ²⁶Jesus answered, "It is he to whom I shall give a piece of bread when I have dipped it." And having dipped the bread, He gave it to Judas Iscariot, the son of Simon.*

The Judas-like people always dip their hands in the same dish you are eating from at the same time you are attempting to eat.

Matthew 26:21-23: ²¹Now as they were eating, He said, "Assuredly, I say to you, one of you will betray Me." ²²And they were exceedingly sorrowful, and each of them began to say to Him, "Lord, is it I?" ²³He answered and said, "He who dipped his hand with Me in the dish will betray Me."

I remember a while ago as I was preparing to teach a leadership class, I was inquiring of the Lord how to know who the Judases are, in general. He responded to me, by saying that Judases tend to always <u>rudely</u> dip (insert) themselves into what you are doing at the same time you are doing something.

That evening during my class, as I began to teach what the Lord had said to me earlier, a person abruptly inserted himself into the teaching attempting rudely to take over the teaching session at the same time I was teaching (feeding) the class. I instantly stopped and let him continue to eat his sup. As the Lord said to me, this is an example of the Judas-like behavior. Judas-like persons tend to take over the same dish from which you are eating. I have seen this type of behavior repeatedly in various forms.

The Lawless One Revealed

2 Thessalonians 2:7-8: *⁷For the mystery of lawlessness is already at work; only He who now restrains will do so until he is **taken** out of the **way**. ⁸And then the lawless one will be revealed, whom the Lord will consume with the breath of His mouth and destroy with the brightness of His coming.*

The mystery of lawlessness will be revealed when "he is **taken** out of the **way**." "**Taken**," in the text above, is translated for the Greek word "ginomai" which means "to birth," "to generate," "to become," to come into being." **"Way"** is translated from the Greek word "mesou," and literally means **"middle."** The phrase "at work" is literally "in-working" (Greek, energeo) a word associated with "energy" (Greek, energia).

Hence the verse literally translates as such: ***"the 'secret' of lawlessness is already 'in-working' ... until he 'births himself' out of the 'middle'."*** How will the mystery of lawlessness, the man of sin, birth himself from the "middle?" He will expose himself by the false energy of Satan! The man of sin will "become" out of the middle by **"showing"** off that he is a god, and **"opposing"** all that is called God, or all that is respected as God! Note: this exposure will occur after the apostasy (the divorce from the true doctrine of Christ). There will be false signs given by Satan that will deceive man to arrogantly oppose God.

This can mean that the "man of sin," in its full force, will only recognize himself as god. All others that are worshipped as God, in the earth, will be rejected by the man of sin. There will also be a **"king"** who "shall do according to his own will: he shall exalt and magnify himself above every god, shall speak blasphemies against the God of gods" **(Daniel 11:36; see also Revelation 13:1-6)**.

"The man of sin" is also the full grown "man" of the sinful nature in those without Christ, and in those who shall betray Christ (Head and Body). This man of sin is revealed in those you may hear say, we don't need to go to Church. Or they may say, "I am god" (this last statement usually comes from **wise merchandisers**—see **Ezekiel 28:1-6**). This kind of attitudes being manifested is the man of sin being revealed.

As previously indicated, another way of understanding what will cause the man of sin, or the secret work of lawlessness, to be birthed from the middle will be the "falling away" (lit., divorce) form God and the faith. The falling away began at the rise of the orthodox religious systems as we know it today. The falling away also includes modern day apostasy from the truth of God—Jesus, the Truth, the Spirit of Truth, and the Word of Truth. (A good example of this apostasy from the doctrine of Jesus Christ is 1 Timothy 6:3-10.)

2 Thessalonians 2:3; 7: *³Let no one deceive you by any means; for …* **unless the falling away comes first,** *and the man of sin is revealed, the son of perdition … ⁶And now you know* **what** *is restraining, that* **he** *may be revealed in his own time. ⁷For the mystery of lawlessness is already at work … until he is 'birthed' out of the 'middle.'*

The "what" that "is restraining" the man of sin's full manifestation; or the "what" that "is restraining" the work of lawlessness full manifestation is the "falling away" that must "come first." After Paul's statement in 2 Thessalonians 2:3-5, Paul then said in the next verse, "And now you know **what** is restraining, that he may be revealed in his own time." How did they know "what" was restraining the mystery of lawlessness from being revealed? Paul had just told them in verses 3 through 5 of 2 Thessalonians.

2 Thessalonians 2:3-6: *³Let no one deceive you by any means;* **for** *… unless the falling away comes first, and the man of sin is revealed, the son of perdition, ⁴who opposes and exalts himself above all that is called God or that is worshiped, so that he sits as God in the temple of God, showing himself that he is God. ⁵Do you not remember that when I was still with you, I told you these things?* **⁶And now you know what is restraining,** *that* **he may be revealed** *in his own time.*

"The falling away" is literally "the divorce," and it is "feminine" in the Greek text. This can mean that there will be a "divorce" from God by some in the Church, who is called a woman or a wife. This is seen in all the religious systems and denominations ("demon-nations") in the world that have fallen away from the truth of God to follow religiosity (outward procession, outward dress, ceremonial observances, and pomp (display). The falling away can be exemplified (defined) as follows:

There is the falling away of the "sect" of the Jewish "religions" (ceremonial observances) by the Pharisees **(Acts 26:5)**. There is the falling away by the **"worship (lit., religion) of angels"** that cheat people of their reward **(Colossians 2:18)**. There is falling away of the **"empty** religion;" religion that ends up in an **"unsuccessful search"** for God's answers **(James 1:12)**.

Note: there is also religion (ceremonial observances) that is pure and not defiled. James said that there is a pure and undefiled religion **(James 1:27)**. We are to ceremonially observe the visitation of widows, the orphans and keeping ourselves unstained by the word.

It follows that there must be a religion (ceremonial observances) that is not pure and that defiles people. There is religion contaminated by the world. There is religion that does not visit the orphans (John 14:18); and the widows (Acts 6:1-4) in their trouble.

Again, there is "pure and undefiled religion," the ceremonial, observances that are acceptable to God. Visiting children bereaved (to deprive by force) in their constrictions is pure and undefiled religion. Visiting divorced women in their constrictions is pure and undefiled religion. Keeping oneself uncontaminated from the world[9] is pure and undefiled religion. *"Pure and undefiled religion before God and the Father is this: to visit*

---

9 The lust of the flesh, the lust of the eyes and pride of life (1 John 2:16)

orphans and widows in their trouble, and to keep oneself unspotted from the world" **(James 1:27).**

There is also the pomp of the outward dress of religious people that is useless. This outward show of long robes, best seats in Church, best seats at feasts, best hotel rooms can be seen in the catholic system and all her daughters (Episcopalians, Lutherans, Presbyterians, etc.); seen in some so-called non-denomination and denominational Churches and seen in other Pentecostal Churches. Listen to Jesus' assessments of this falling away through religious observances.

Luke 20:46-47: ⁴⁶*"Beware of the scribes, who desire to go around in* **long robes, love greetings** *in the marketplaces, the* **best seats in the synagogues,** *and the* **best places** *at feasts,* ⁴⁷*"who devour widows' houses, and for a pretense make long prayers. These will receive* **greater condemnation."**

There will also be a prevalence of divorce in the Church (leaders and lay people alike) and the world, a sign that the falling away is still at work. Remember, the falling away literally means "to divorce." It is feminine of "the writing of a divorce" *(Matthew 5:31).*

Women will be divorcing their husbands, and husbands will be divorcing their wives. Isaiah also says that "the wicked is like the **'divorced'** sea" **(Isaiah 57:20).** The sea of humanity has and will divorce itself from the living God.

This is a result of religious systems (mystery Babylon) that have divorced God and will divorce God to be remarried to the world, the beast, and its system. Most of the orthodox Churches in the world (China included) are "State sponsored" — the governments pay their bills and salaries.

Sad to say some of the so-called independent Churches are also largely supported by the governments system. In Revelation 17:7, the religious system of mystery Babylon is **"carried"** (sustained, declared, received, based)[10] by the governmental system of a beast (sad to say that this is the push of some evangelical circles). This divorce from God (the falling away) by the apostate Church is now the norm; and those who follow "the truth of God" are being persecuted by those who have fallen away.

In conclusion of the chapter, I would like to give a note of balance here. Nehemiah and Ezra were also temporarily supported by the government of their time. Yet, there is mystery Babylon who is sustained by the beast that has a negative connotation **(Revelation 17:16).**

There are also true believers who obtain some wealth from some governmental system like Ezra, Nehemiah, and the children of Israel when they left Egypt, and so on. True relationship with Jesus determines the difference! Yet, be mindful that one of the high priests who sentenced Jesus to death was appointed by the fourth beast of Daniel, Rome; and the other high priest was also sanctioned by Rome.

---

[10] As defined by Strong's Concordance NT #941 and #939 in Revelation 17:7.

The Lawless Energy of Satan

*2 Thessalonians 2:7-11: ⁷For the mystery of lawlessness is already at work ... ⁸... the lawless one will be revealed, whom the Lord will consume with the breath of His mouth and destroy with the brightness of His coming. ⁹The coming of [the lawless one] is according to **the working (lit energy) of Satan**, with all power, signs, and lying wonders, ¹⁰and with all unrighteous deception among those who perish, because they did not receive the love of the truth, that they might be saved. ¹¹And for this reason God will send them **strong delusion (lit., energy of error)**, that they should believe **the lie.***

The word "energy" (energia) is used eight (8) times in the Scriptures. There is God's energy. There is Jesus' energy. There is energy of the body of Christ. There is energy of Satan. There is the energy of error.

"The 'energy' of [God's] mighty 'force'" ***(Eph 1:19)***

"The 'energy' of [God's] power" ***(Eph 3:7)***

"The 'energy' by which every part [of the Body] does its share" ***(Eph 4:16)***

"The 'energy' by which [Jesus] is able even to subdue all things to Himself" ***(Philip 3:21)***

"[God's] 'energy' which 'in-work' in [us] 'in power'" ***(Col 1:29)***

"You also were raised with [Jesus] through faith in the 'energy' of God" ***(Col 2:12)***

"The coming ... is according to the 'energy' of Satan" ***(2 Thess 2:9)***

"God shall send them 'energy of error' that they should believe the lie" ***(2 Thess 2:11)***

According to the Scriptures references at the beginning of this section, the lawless one (or the wicked one) being revealed is also linked to "the energy of Satan." This energy of Satan has several aspects that must be discussed.

2 Thessalonians 2:3-4, KJV: ³… *That man of sin* …⁴*Who opposes and exalts himself above all that is called God, or that is worshipped; so that he as God sits in the temple of God,* **shewing himself that he is God.**

Acts 2:22, KJV: *Ye men of Israel, hear these words; Jesus of Nazareth, a man* **approved** *(showed) of God among you* **by miracles and wonders and signs, which** *God did by him in the midst of you, as ye yourselves also know.*

2 Thessalonians 2:8-10, KJV: ⁸*And then shall that Wicked be revealed, whom the Lord shall consume with the spirit of his mouth and shall destroy with the brightness of his coming:* ⁹*[Even him,] whose coming is after the* **working (lit., energy) of Satan with all power and signs and lying wonders.** ¹⁰*And with all deceivableness of unrighteousness in them that perish; because they received not the love of the truth, that they might be saved.*

The man of sin will **"show"** himself that he is a god." As we learned earlier, he will **show** himself to be a god by mimicking "The God." How will the man of sin mimic God? He will "show" similar miraculous works like Jesus.

Jesus was **"showed"** to be of God "by **miracles, and wonders, and signs."** So likewise, the man of sin will **"show"** himself as a god, by the energy of Satan **"in all power, signs, and wonders of falsehood and in all 'cheating of unrighteousness.'"** Yes, the "energy of Satan" can produce "power" which **source** is out of falsehood.

Yes, the energy of Satan can produce "signs" which **source** is out of "falsehood!" The "energy of Satan" can produce "wonders" which source is also out of "falsehood!" The "energy of Satan" can produce "cheating" which **source** is out of "falsehood." And some will believe these lying demonstrations which come out of the sinful nature are legitimate.

As one studies the Greek text, one will see that the word "lying," which is better translated as "pseudo," "falsehood" or "lie" is "genitive" in "case." "Genitive case" shows the **"source."** The "source" of Satan's power is "falsehood." The source of Satan's signs is falsehood. The source of Satan's wonders is falsehood. The source of Satan's ability to make a person "cheat" is falsehood.

Yet, it is **God** who dispatches this "energy of Satan" also called the "energy of error." Yes, the energy of Satan, the energy of error, is dispatched by God.[11] Why does God allow this false energy? He allows it that those who refuse to believe the love of the truth may believe "the lie." "And for this cause **God** shall send them **strong delusion (lit., energy of error)**, that they should believe **a lie (lit., the lie)."** The energy of Satan sways the deceived to the "error" of believing the lie.

What is the lie? The lie is idol worship! The lie is creature worship, rather than worshipping the "Creator"! The "work of lawlessness" is "the lie" manifested in unshapely sexual orientations, as we will see in a later section.

2 Thessalonians 2:10-11, KJV: [10]*... Because they received not the **love of the truth**, that they might be saved.* [11]*And for this cause **God** shall send them **strong delusion (lit., energy of error)**, that they should believe **a lie (lit., the lie)**.*

Here is an example of a false sign of idol worship. Recently, it was said that a six-arm child was born in India that favored one of their gods. The Bible said that people become whatever they worship **(compare Psalm 135:15-18)**. In this case, the worship of the six-arm god produced a false sign of a six-arm child through the energy of Satan, or through the energy of error.

I am quite sure, as the Scriptures has predicted, they will continue to believe the lie that a manmade object is indeed a god, because of the false sign of six-arm child that looks like their

---

11 Compare 2 Chronicles 18:19-22

manmade god. As Paul predicted, the sinful nature has showed itself to be a god by a false sign. "And for this reason, God will send them **'energy of error,'** that they should believe **the lie."** **(2 Thessalonians 2:11, KJV).**

Revelation 13:11-15, KJV: ¹¹*And I beheld another beast coming up out of the earth; and he had two horns like a lamb, and he spoke as a dragon.* ¹²*And he exercises all the power of the first beast before him and causes the earth and them which dwell therein to worship the first beast, whose deadly wound was healed.* ¹³***And he doeth great 'signs,' so that he makes fire come down from heaven on the earth in the sight of men,*** ¹⁴*And deceives them that dwell on the earth by the means of those 'signs' which he had power to do in the sight of the beast; saying to them that dwell on the earth, that they should make an image to the beast, which had the wound by a sword, and did live.* ¹⁵*And he had power to give **'spirit'** unto the image of the beast,* ***that the image of the beast should both speak, and cause that as many as would not worship the image of the beast should be killed.***

The Cause of the Energy of Error

2 Thessalonians 2:10-11: [10]... **Because they did not receive the love of the truth**, *that they might be saved.* [11]*And* **for this reason** *God will send them 'energy of errors,' that they should believe 'the lie.'*

What is the "reason" of the lawless energy which leads to the work of lawlessness? The cause is that "**they did not receive the love of the truth** that they might be saved." Yes, <u>not</u> receiving "the love" that comes from "the truth" is the reason God Himself will send the un-persuadable ones the energy of error, which is the energy of Satan. Thus, we must understand what "the love" is; and what "the truth" is?

John 14:6: Jesus said to him, **"I am** *the way,* **the truth,** *and the life. No one comes to the Father except through Me."*

Romans 1:24-25: Therefore, God also gave them up to uncleanness, in the lusts of their hearts, to dishonor their bodies among themselves, [25] *who exchanged* **the truth of God** *for* **the lie and worshiped** *and served the creature rather than the Creator, who is blessed forever.*

Jesus is the truth; and there is also "the truth of God." Thus, when someone does not "receive the love of the truth," it can mean that they did not receive Jesus; and it can mean that they do not receive "the truth of God" that God is to be "worshipped and served." Some will "exchange the truth of God to worship and serve the creature rather than the Creator (God)." God is to be worshipped! We are <u>not</u> to worship created things. Yet, some have opposed the worship of God, which is "the truth of God." This refusal to worship God by some of the Romans Paul wrote to sounds familiar to 2 Thessalonians 2.

2 Thessalonians 2:3-4: [3]*Let no one deceive you by any means; for that Day will not come unless ... the man of sin is revealed ... who opposes and* **exalts himself above all** *that is called God* **or that is worshiped....**

"The Truth" is Jesus. "The Spirit is Truth." God's Word is truth! "The truth" is also that God is to be worshipped as the Creator. We also have to **"receive** the love of **the truth."** We have to receive the "Spirit of truth." We have to receive the Father's love for us and worship Him for His love. We have to receive Jesus' love for us and worship Him!

For those who "oppose" the worship of the Father and reject "the love" of Jesus, there is a danger of being given over to believe the lie. Rather, we must receive "the love of the truth!" We must receive "the love" of "the truth of God" that God is to be "worshipped and served." With that said, let us now look at "the love" to gain an understanding of why we must receive this love of God.

1 John 3:16: By this we know ***love (lit., the love),*** *because He laid down His life for us. And we also ought to lay down our lives for the brethren.*

John 15:13: Greater love has no one than this, than to lay down one's life for his friends.

In this verse "the love" is defined as Jesus laying down His life for us; and the truth that we must also lay down our life for our brothers and sisters in the Lord Jesus. John emphatically said that "**by this** we know **'the love.'**" "By" what do we know the love? "The truth" that Jesus really laid down His life for us approximately 2,000 years ago; and that Jesus picked up His life again in His Resurrection for our justification.

1 John 4:10: In this is ***love (lit., the love),*** *not that we loved God, but that He loved us and sent His Son to be the propitiation for our sins.*

Here is another definition of "the love." "[God] loved us and sent His Son to be the **propitiation** for our sins." The word "propitiation" is from a root that means mercy, graciousness, cheerful. It is in the same word family that is also translated as "propitiation" and the "Mercy Seat" **(1 John 2:1-2 w/Hebrews 9:5).**

Jesus is our "Atonement" for all our sins, present, past, and future. Jesus is our Mercy Seat personified. Thus, "the love" is also the truth that Jesus is our Mercy Seat with regards to "all manner of sins." We must always "believe" that He is full of mercy towards us; and that we must also "receive" His mercy for us.

*1 John 4:16: And we have known and **believed the love** that God has for us. God is love, and he who abides in love abides in God, and God in him.*

2 Thessalonians 2:10b-11: [10]*... Because they **did not receive the love of the truth**, that they might be saved.* [11]*And **for this reason** God will send them strong delusion, that they should believe the lie.*

It is serious to "<u>not</u> receive the love" that comes from "the truth." Jesus is the truth **(John 14:6).** We just learned that "the love" is Jesus laying down His life for us; and that He is our Atonement (Mercy Seat) for sins.

If any refuse to receive "the love," God will eventually give that person over to the energy of error. The energy of error is the energy of Satan's that deceives by false powers, wonders, and signs. God's judgment against refusing "the love of the truth" gets even stronger. God dispatches this judgment of the energy of deceiving "that they should believe **the lie:** that they all may **be condemned** ...."

We all have to receive "the love" that comes from "the truth." Yet, there are some who think they are unforgivable. This attitude is far from the truth. The truth is all manner of sins are forgivable, except for one type of blasphemy.

*Matthew 12:31: Therefore, I say to you, **every sin and blasphemy will be forgiven men,** but the blasphemy against the Spirit will not be forgiven men.*

I implore you, receive the love of the truth that Jesus has already laid down His life (died) for our sins! All sins are forgivable except one! With that understood, let also not reject Jesus' love by foolishly believing that God will reinstitute animal sacrifice again. **We do not need animal sacrifices any more to be forgiven.**

"For it is not possible that the blood of bulls and goats could take away sins" **(Hebrews 10:4).** He put away animal sacrifices once and for all. It is against the sacrifice of Jesus to institute any animal sacrifice again. Through Jesus, God did away with animal sacrifices forever. Our redemption is eternal! "Christ is become of no effect to you, whosoever of you are justified by the law; you are fallen from grace" **(Galatians 5:4, KJV)**.

Hebrews 9:11-14: ¹¹*But Christ came as High Priest of the good things to come, with the greater and more perfect tabernacle not made with hands, that is, not of this creation.* ¹²***Not with*** *the blood of goats and calves, but **with His own blood** He entered the Most Holy Place **once for all**, having obtained eternal redemption.* ¹³*For if the blood of bulls and goats and the ashes of a heifer, sprinkling the unclean, sanctifies for the purifying of the flesh,* ¹⁴*how much more shall the blood of Christ, who through the eternal Spirit offered Himself without spot to God, cleanse your conscience from dead works to serve the living God?*

Again, there are some, so called believers in the earth today (2011), who do not believe there are forgiven or forgivable for some past mistakes. Thus, they continue to sin worse and worse. These things ought not to be so.

We have the free gift of "the love" of Jesus (the truth). All we have to do is accept Jesus atonement for us by faith. I beg you; believe in the good news of Jesus Christ! Believe in His love for us! Believe in His mercy! Believe in His atonement for our sins! Do not reject the offering of God given for our benefit.

Rejection of "the love" of Jesus ("the truth") can be detrimental to your life. God Himself gets personally involved with those who reject His love. "Because they did not receive the love of the truth … for this reason **God** will send (lit., dispatch) them strong delusion (lit., energy of error), that they should believe the lie" **(see 2 Thessalonians 2:10-11).**

*Romans 1:25-26: [25]Who exchanged the truth of God for the lie and worshiped and served the creature rather than the Creator, who is blessed forever. Amen. [26]For this reason **God** gave them up to vile passions.*

The references above are strong. God Himself gets involved when people reject His love. There is a judgment in this life — it is called being deceived into believing the lie; and there is a "judgment" in the future.

God sends this judgment of the energy of error "that they should believe the lie;" **and** "that they all may **be condemned** …." The Lord Jesus said something similar about those who would reject Him. "He who rejects Me, and does not receive My words, has that which judges him — the word that I have spoken **will judge him in the last day"** *(John 12:48).* I beg you "receive the love of the truth" (Jesus' propitiation for us)!

*Ephesians 3:14-19: [14]For this cause I bow my knees unto the Father of our Lord Jesus Christ, [15]Of whom the whole family in heaven and earth is named, [16]That he would grant you, according to the riches of his glory, to be strengthened with might by his Spirit in the inner man; [17]That Christ may dwell in your hearts by faith; that you, being rooted and grounded in **love**, [18]May be able to comprehend with all saints what is the breadth, and length, and depth, and height; [19]**And to know the love of Christ, which passes knowledge**, that you might be filled with all the fulness of God.*

The Lie Defined

2 Thessalonians 2:10-11: *¹⁰… Because they did not receive the love of the truth, that they might be saved. ¹¹And for this reason God will send them strong delusion, that they should believe* **the lie.**

Romans 1:25-26: *²⁵Who exchanged the truth of God for* **the lie and** *worshiped and served the creature rather than the Creator, who is blessed forever. Amen. ²⁶For this reason God gave them up to vile passions.*

"The lie" encompasses different dimensions. "The lie" is Satan "speaking out of his own." "The lie" is to worship manmade things instead of God—the Creator. "The lie" is to worship creatures (created things) instead of the Creator. "The lie" is same-sex orientation; or pansexual orientation (i.e., lesbianism and same-gender relationships, etc.).[12] Let us look at each of the items listed above individually.

"The lie" is the Devil speaking out of his own

John 8:44: … The Devil … **abode not in the truth,** *because there is no truth in him. When he speaks* **a lie (the lie),** *he speaks* **of (lit., out of) his own ….**

Dr. Joshua (Turnel) Nelson of Trinidad said to us before his passing that **"God cannot lie."** He also said, "The Devil cannot speak truth." He said that "only humans can both tell a lie and tell truth." Dr. Nelson emphasized that we must tell the truth; if a person pastors twenty people, do not lie and say that you pastor thirty.

"The lie" of the Devil is contrary to the truth of Jesus. Jesus said that any person who speaks from his own, seeks his own glory **(John 7:18).** Thus, the lie of the Devil is that he seeks his own glory

---

[12] Note: This does not mean that we treat people bad because of their sexual orientation. As Christian we are to love them asking the Spirit of the Father to grant them repentance!

by speaking from his own self. Our Lord Jesus is opposite Satan. Jesus said that **"He [Jesus] does nothing of Himself" (John 5:19; 30)."** Jesus only does what He sees His Father does. This means that Jesus did nothing that **originated** from himself.

John 5:30, KJV: ***I can of mine own self do nothing****: as I hear, I judge: and my judgment is just; because **I seek not mine own will**, but the will of the Father which hath sent me.*

Every single thing that Jesus did was because the heavenly Father told Him to do it; or because He saw His Father do it **(John 5:19).** In other words, Jesus' statement is talking about absolute reliance on God's approval to do a task before the task is embarked upon. Jesus did absolutely **nothing** on His own. Jesus is the truth, personified.

"The lie" is to worship manmade objects instead of God

Romans 1:21-23; 25: ²¹*Because, although they knew God, they did not glorify Him as God, nor were thankful, but became futile in their thoughts, and their foolish hearts were darkened.* ²²*Professing to be wise, they became fools,* ²³*and changed the glory of the incorruptible God into an image **made** like corruptible man—and birds and four-footed animals and creeping things …*²⁵ *who exchanged the truth of God for **the lie and** worshiped and served the creature rather than the Creator, who is blessed forever. Amen.*

In the verse above we see that mankind "change the glory of the incorruptible God into an image **made** like corruptible man—and birds and four-footed animals and creeping things." Mankind did not glorify God as God even though "they knew God;" thus, they made their own gods to worship and serve (revelation 13:11-15).

Mankind decided to change who they wanted worship or glorify. Mankind decided to worship (glorify) "an image **made**;" the "made" image of man, birds, creeping animals, etcetera. Saying it another way, mankind who refused to retain God in their knowledge, decided in their own wisdom to worship "images" they "made."

"The lie" is worshipping images made to look like corruptible man and images made to look like animals (i.e., Buddha (manlike), some of the gods of India (manlike and animal-like), the beast of Revelation 13, etc.). The Lord said "fools" worship an image that they themselves craft with their own hands.

The same material they use to make their idol-gods, they use for corruptible purposes. The wood some isolators use to make their idol, they use the same wood to heat themselves and cook their food. Yet the idols makers and idol worshippers do not even consider how foolish this is **(See Isaiah 44:9-20).**

"The lie" is to worship creatures instead of the Creator

Romans 1:19-22; 25: [19]*Because what may be known of God is manifest* ***in them,*** *for God has shown it to them.* [20]*For since the creation of the world His invisible attributes are clearly seen, being understood by the things that are made, even His eternal power and Godhead, so that they are without excuse,* [21]*because, although they knew God, they did not glorify Him as God, nor were thankful, but became futile in their thoughts, and their foolish hearts were darkened.* [22]*Professing to be wise, they became fools ...* [25] *who exchanged the truth of God for* ***the lie and*** *worshiped* ***and served the creature rather than the Creator****, who is blessed forever. Amen.*

I remember as a young boy in Jamaica, West Indies, I was walking on the walkway a jot passed the gate leading into the property. At that moment it appears that I was transfixed between heaven and earth; and I looked up and said, "Surely there must be a God." That was God revealing Himself to me at a young age. At that time, I was not brought up in Church; however, I realized there must be a Creator at a young age. The Creator's name is Jesus; and I began praying to Him at a young age in Jamaica West Indies; and by the time I was 24 years of age, Jesus became my Savior, Lord, King, Priest, Apostle, Baptizer, etc.

God reveals Himself **in** every creature **(Romans 10:18; Colossians 1:23).** "Because what may be known of God is manifest **in them,** for **God** has shown it to them" **(Romans 1:19).** However, mankind still insists on creature worship. This creature worship is defined as "the lie." The Devil fathered "the lie" of both man and angels (created beings) worshiping him (who is also a created beings); the lie of worshipping his idols (manmade images); and the lie of worshipping animals (also created things), **instead of fearing and worshipping God (the Creator).**

The serpent spoke of (out of) his "own" self **(John 8:44).** He also spoke of his own worship **(Luke 4:6-8).** He caused other created things—angels and men—to worship him instead of worshipping the Christ.

*Romans 1:25, NIV: They exchanged the truth of God for **a lie (lit; the lie)** and worshiped and served **created things** rather than the Creator – who is forever praised. Amen.*

Paul said that anyone who "exchanged the truth of God for the lie" is the same as one who "worshiped and served the **created things** rather than the **Creator.**" "Although they claimed to be wise, they became fools and exchanged the glory of the immortal God for images made to look like mortal man and birds and animals and reptiles" **(Romans 1:22-23, NIV).**

"The lie," according to Romans 1:25 quoted above, is when the created things (mankind/angels) worship other created things, which can range from excessive love of animals to worshipping humans and human body parts. In Revelation 13 the people worshipped the "dragon"—a "reptile" and the "beast"—a four footed animal, and the beast's image. The worship of the beast and his image points to the worship of beastly man (666) and man's governmental systems that are anti-God **(see Daniel 7).**

In Revelation 13, they worshipped the "image of the beast", which in the words of the NIV in Romans 1:23, is "images made to look … animals." As you can see, Revelation 13 lines up with Romans 1:23 perfectly, it does not stop there. Paul said in the book of Romans that God eventually gave over the creature worshipers to dishonor their bodies by mimicking what they were doing to these idols. Creature worshipping creature became man in man and woman with woman.

"The lie" is same-sex orientation

Romans 1:25-27: *25who **exchanged** the truth of God for the lie and worshiped and served the creature rather than the Creator, who is blessed forever. Amen. 26 For this reason God gave them up to vile passions. For even their women **exchanged the natural use for what is against nature**. 27 **Likewise** also **the men, leaving the natural use of the woman, burned in their lust for one another, men with men** committing what is shameful ....*

Historically, same-sex began in the invisible and then manifested in the visible. Life on earth is like a symmetric object with a line of axis in the middle. On one side of the axis — the line between visible and invisible — there is a spiritual reality. On the other side of the axis, there is a symmetric natural reality.

In other words, same-sex is a mirror exposure of something that happened historically in the invisible. Same-sex is a mirror of creature worship and worship of manmade objects. Same-sex is "the lie."

Romans 1:24-25: *24Therefore God also gave them up to uncleanness, in the lusts of their hearts, to dishonor their bodies among themselves, 25who exchanged the truth of God for **the lie,** and worshiped and served the creature rather than the Creator, who is blessed forever. Amen.*

*John 8:44: You are of your father the devil, and the desires of your father you want to do. He was a murderer from the beginning, and does not stand in the truth, because there is no truth in him. When he speaks **a (Gk., the) lie,** he speaks from his own resources, for he is a liar and the **father** of it.*

The Devil **fathered** some things. One of them is "the lie." However, what is "the lie?" As we learned earlier, humans are famous for worshipping "creatures," including human creatures and animal creatures. Again, this is "the lie." Worshiping the creature instead of The Creator is the lie. Worshipping the creature instead of the Creator is spiritually a replica of same sex relationship. We also call it same-gender relationships and lesbianism. Allow me to explain.

Satan fathered the lie. Thus, according to Romans 1:25, he is the source of creature (animal) admiration. Remember he is also a serpent (beast), and he instituted satanic worship. Jesus stated that "he [Satan] speaks "'the' lie." In other words, he [Satan] caused other angels—creatures—to worship him [a creature].

God says that creature worshipping creature is the lie. The same God also states that creature worshipping creature results in same-sex. In other words, when the other created beings worshipped Satan, a created being, in God's opinion, it was the same as a same-sex act.

In the world today men worship men, women worship women, men worship women and women worship men. Men worship women's body parts—buttocks, thighs, faces, noses, eye colors, hair, breast, etc. Women worship men's body parts. Humans worship human basketball players, human football players, human soccer players, human tennis players, human hockey players, human historical figures, and men's mind.

The arenas are filled with the indulgers. There is also same-sex in the Church. The fathers/mothers in the Church are being worshipped by the sons/daughters. The result of this kind of male and female worship is sexual sins, leaders of the Church sleeping with the congregation, and some of their spiritual sons and daughters.

Categorically, the majority of athletes and famous people whom other humans worship usually fall into sexual sins. Categorically, "man worship" in the Church is generating sexual sins, to include but not limited to, same-sex. They indulge in all manner of dishonorable sex that ranges from adultery-sex, mentors with mentees having sex, and so on. All one has to do is listen to or read the news carefully.

The reason for this kind of human behavior is that mankind refused to retain the Creator in their minds. Instead, humanity worships the very thing that they are—a created being. **Man was created to worship the Creator, not the creature.** Creature worshipping creature results in "the lie" of same-sex.

Romans 1:25-27: *25who **exchanged** the truth of God for the lie and worshiped and served the creature rather than the Creator, who is blessed forever. Amen. 26For this reason God gave them up to vile passions. For even their women **exchanged** the natural use for what is against nature. 27**Likewise** also the men, leaving the natural use of the woman, burned in their lust for one another, men with men....*

Paul taught that since mankind **"exchanged** the truth of God for the lie ... for this reason ... their women **exchanged** their natural use ... likewise also the men." We see here the symmetry. Since humans decided to "exchange" the worship of God for creature worship (a spices worshipping the "same" spices); God gave them up to "exchange" their sexual orientation to become same-sex (same gender-sex).

The word homosexuality has a Greek etymology. **"Homo"** is a Greek word that means **"same." "Sex"** means a division of gender or species. Satan is a species of creature. We call them angels. Angel species worshiping angel species is a spiritual homosexual act.

They are the **SAME** creature **SPECIES** worshiping each other. The sign that there is an abundance of creature worship on the earth is the prevalence and acceptance of same-sex behavior. Men have made their own image a god. Man has made the image of animal—a creature—a god.

Most animals were made to eat and to have fun with. They were not made to be worshipped. Man was made to dominate the animal kingdom, not to worship creatures. The images of beasts and the images of men are now the idols of this age. The result is the uncleanness of same-sex.

All of the manifestation of same-sex is a result of the spirit of Satan causing creature worship. Satan went against God's physics when he caused this lie. Satan and mankind gave their back to God and worshipped each other. Thus, God gave them over to practice sex which is against "physics" — men in men and women with women.

Romans 1:24-27: [24] *Therefore God also gave them up to uncleanness, in the lusts of their hearts, to dishonor their bodies among themselves,* [25]*who exchanged* **the truth of God** *for* **the lie,** *and worshiped and served the creature rather than the Creator, who is blessed forever. Amen.* [26]*For this reason God gave them up to vile passions. For even their women exchanged the* **natural (Gk., physical or physics)** *use for what is against* **nature (Gk., growth).** [27]*Likewise also the men, leaving the* **natural (Gk., physical or physics)** *use of the woman, burned in their lust for one another, men* **with (lit., in)** *men committing what is shameful, and receiving in themselves the penalty of their error which was due.*

Creature worshipping creature was **not** the spiritual or physical relationship that God intended. His intent **is** for creature to worship Creator (Jesus). The physics of the true worship of God always works.

The Work of Lawlessness Defined

*Matthew 7:23: And then I will declare to them, 'I never knew you; depart from Me, you who **practice lawlessness (lit., work lawlessness)**!'*

*2 Peter 2:8: For that righteous man, dwelling among them, tormented his righteous soul from day to day by seeing and hearing their **lawless deeds (lit., lawless works)**.*

*2 Thessalonians 2:7: For the mystery of **lawlessness is already at work (lit., already in-work the lawlessness)** ....*

The works of lawlessness are the works of "the lie" that produces "all power 'even' signs 'even' wonders of falsehood." There are apparently two sources of miraculous powers in the earth, God, and Satan. Satan pseudo power is **not** equal to God, because Satan's power is "derived."

Saying another way, the sources of power appears to be either from "the truth" or from "the lie." The works of lawlessness includes power that flows from falsehood (the lie); signs that flow from falsehood (the lie) and wonders that flow from falsehood (the lie).

Jesus was the first to give the clue as to the source of certain acts of powers. The apostle Paul and Peter also gave an understanding concerning "the lie" that can eventually produce false powers, signs, and wonders. We will start with Jesus' revelation first.

*Matthew 7:21-23: ²¹"Not everyone who says to Me, 'Lord, Lord,' shall enter the kingdom of heaven, but he who does the will of My Father in heaven. ²²"Many will say to Me in that day, 'Lord, Lord, have we not prophesied in Your name, cast out demons in Your name, and done many wonders in Your name?'" ²³"And then I will declare to them, 'I never knew you; depart from Me, you who **practice (lit., work) lawlessness!'"***

In the verse above, there will be some folks who claimed that Jesus was/is their Lord; and that they worked miracles through the name of Jesus. They claimed to prophesy in the name of Jesus. They claimed to cast out demons in the name of Jesus. They also claimed to have "done many wonders" in the name of Jesus. However, Jesus had a different "take" on their claims.

Jesus emphatically declared that He did not know them; and that they "'worked' lawlessness" (Greek: "**ergazomenoi ten anomian**"). The combined use of an inflection of "ergon" (work) and "anomia" (lawlessness) are use in two other significant texts. In 2 Thessalonians 2:7, there is a mystery of the "in-work of lawlessness." In 2 Peter 2:8, he indicated that there are "lawless works."

Thus, lawlessness can be "worked" in a person "internally;" in the words of Paul there is the "in-work of the lawlessness." Peter then takes it a little further and defined "lawless works as sodomy;" and as you will see "lawless works" of sodomy is linked to "the lie."

*2 Peter 2:4-8: ⁴For if God did **not spare the angels** who sinned, but cast them down to hell and delivered them into chains of darkness, to be reserved for judgment; ⁵and did not spare the ancient world, but saved Noah, one of eight people, a preacher of righteousness, bringing in the flood on the world of the ungodly; ⁶ and turning the cities of **Sodom and Gomorrah** into ashes, condemned them to destruction, making them an example to those who afterward would live ungodly; ⁷and delivered righteous Lot, who was oppressed by the filthy conduct of the wicked ⁸(for that righteous man, dwelling among them, tormented his righteous soul from day to day by seeing and hearing **their lawless deeds**).*

According to Jude, the angels referenced above in 2 Peter are the angels who fell from their first home to sleep with humans (women). This is an act the Bible, in Jude, defines as "going after **strange** flesh." The angels in Peter's writing are also linked to the "filthy conduct" of Sodom and Gomorrah. These acts of the angels and the men of Sodom and Gomorrah are called "lawless deeds" by Peter

*Jude 1:6-7: ⁶And the **angels** who did not keep their proper domain, but left their own abode, He has reserved in everlasting chains under darkness for the judgment of the great day; ⁷as Sodom and Gomorrah, and the cities around them in a similar manner to these, having given themselves over to **sexual immorality** and **gone after strange flesh**, are set forth as an example, suffering the vengeance of eternal fire.*

Sodom's and Gomorrah's "lawless works" varied. Jude said they went after strange flesh. The Greek text reads that they went **"behind** different flesh." One does not have to think too hard to conclude what Jude meant by "different flesh" and "behind." Genesis 19 tells us that in Sodom and Gomorrah men were sleeping with men. They also wanted to sleep with two (2) of the elect angels that came to destroy those cities. According to Ezekiel, Sodom also did other lawless works.

*Ezekiel 16:49-50: Look, this was the iniquity of your sister Sodom: She and her daughter had **pride, fullness of food,** and **abundance of idleness; neither did she strengthen the hand of the poor and needy**. And they were **haughty** and **committed abomination** before Me; therefore, I took them away as I saw fit.*

The "abomination' of Sodom is the lawless works of same-sex acts **(Genesis 19).** It must also be understood that from same-sex acts (a facet of the lie) the potential is there for false signs, wonders, and miracles to work. There are many in the Body of Christ today who have not allowed the Lord to deliver them from the lie. Here are the stages that lead to walking in "the lie."

Mankind refuse to receive the love of the truth; or mankind refuse to retain God in their knowledge **(2 Thessalonians 2:10; Romans 1:28; 1:19-20).**

Mankind then begins to walk in the first stages of the lie—they worship manmade things and creatures (humans and animals); they oppose all that is called God **(2 Thessalonians 2:3-4; Romans 23-25).**

Since mankind receive not the love of the truth, God then gives them over to the "energy of error" to believe the lie **(2 Thessalonians 2:11).**

Those who refuse the love of the truth, those who reject the truth of God is the given over to another stage of the lie—dishonoring their bodies among themselves—men in men and women with women **(Romans 1:27).**

There is also another stage in the works of lawlessness, a stage where false signs are given to those who practice same-sex, and so on by which they justify their lawless deeds; and the final stage is when the man of lawlessness is exposed (revealed) through false sings being produced by "the energy of Satan." **(Revelation 16:13-14; 2 Thessalonians 2:9 w/2:4; Matthew 7:21-23)**

Herein are the deceptions of the lie. If mankind (saved or unsaved) continues to reject God's love and God's truth, God will send them a strong energy of error, the energy of Satan, to work false sings, false wonders, false miracles, etc. These false indicators will deceive the deceived into believing that their lawless actions are acceptable by God. (These are some of the people who are always looking for signs as confirmation.)

They will also think that the miracles being worked through them is indeed God in their temple showing Himself to be God; when in reality, it is the mature man of sin through satanic energy performing these false indicators. **In other words, lifestyle determines what source miraculous power, wonders and signs come from.**

There are some who go about believing that walking in the lie (worshiping of made and created things) is acceptable to God. The answer is no! Creature worship and worship of manmade objects are not acceptable. There are also those who say, I am not an idol worshipper; yet they have the other form of the lie working in their lives—the lie of same sex. Same-sex is the work of lawlessness also.

The common vernacular is "He is a loving God, and He understands my sexual orientation. I was born that way." Or some may say that "as long as I believe in Jesus, I am okay, my sexual orientation does not matter to God."

God does indeed love the person whose sexual orientation has been distorted in the hope that they change; however, He "hates lawlessness" **(Hebrews 1:9).** Anyway, a person looks at it, misrepresentation of sexual orientation is a result of sin; and the Bible defines sin as lawlessness.

In God Word, same-sex has its origin in idol worship and same-sex is the works of lawlessness. Remember, the worship of a human is a rejection of "the truth of God," and this rejection of God is idol worship. The worship of animals is also a rejection of God and is also idol worship. And according to God, same sex comes from the fact that mankind refuse to retain God in their knowledge.

Mankind refuses to receive the love of the truth. Thus, somewhere in humanity's history, God gave over some to commit the dishonorable act of the lie, same-sex. It follows that God Himself also allowed false indicators to occur to deceive the deceived even more.

Finally, there are Churches in the world that were founded by men and women with homosexual lifestyle, lesbian lifestyle, and bisexual lifestyle. Thus, some have permitted the lie to take root (founded) as acceptable in their congregations. They have done what Joshua (Jesus) said not to do.

They have laid a different foundation of "the fragrance of the moon" (Jericho) in their firstborns, rather than laying the foundation of the firstborn, Jesus, Christ **(see 1 Kings 15:34 w/Joshua 6:26).** These foundations of the "fragrance of the moon" (fragrance of the rulers of darkness) have to be removed and the foundation of Jesus Christ has to be laid properly **(1 Corinthians 3:11).**

God **does** want to wash and clean the homosexuals, lesbians, bisexuals, catamites, etc. **(1 Corinthians 6:9-11).** However, they cannot be washed or made clean by those who have founded Churches with the belief that "the lie," is acceptable to God. The dangerous thing about same-sex orientation is that false prophesy, pseudo casting out of demons, false miracles, false wonders, and false miraculous power flows comes from the lie.

Matthew 7:23: And then I will declare to them, 'I never knew you; depart from Me, you who **practice lawlessness (lit., work lawlessness)!'**

2 Peter 2:8: For that righteous man, dwelling among them, tormented his righteous soul from day to day by seeing and hearing their **lawless deeds (lit., lawless works).**

2 Thessalonians 2:7: For the mystery of **lawlessness is already at work (lit., already in-work the lawlessness)** ....

Signs of Demons

Revelation 16:13-14: *¹³And I saw* **three unclean spirits** *like frogs coming out of the mouth of the dragon, out of the mouth of the beast, and out of the mouth of the false prophet.* *¹⁴For* **they are spirits of demons, performing signs**, *which go out to the kings of the earth and of the whole world, to gather them to the battle of that great day of God Almighty.*

Here is a question for our age, can demons and/or Satan work sings, wonders, and acts of powers?

In the text above we see that spirits have the ability to multiply themselves. In addition, we see "unclean spirits" or "spirits of demons **performing** signs." "Performing" is from the Greek word "poieo" from which we get our English words poem, poet, and poetry. "Poieo" literally means to do, to produce, to make, construct, and form.

Thus, the spirits of demons "'produced signs.' They "constructed signs." They "formed signs." They also "made' signs," and they also "'did' signs." Yes, demons can "'perform' signs." There are also "powers of the enemy." Or there are invisible beings that are called "powers;" and they also perform power acts.

However, Jesus will continue to rule until these "power enemies" are put under His feet. "Then comes the end, when He delivers the kingdom to God the Father, when He puts an end to all rule and all authority and **power.** For He must reign till He has put all **enemies** under His feet" **(1 Corinthians 15:24-25).**

Luke 10:19: Behold, I give you the authority to trample on serpents and scorpions, and over all the **power of the enemy,** *and nothing shall by any means* **hurt** *you.*

The enemies of the Church have **powers**. In fact, some of the spirits are called **"powers."** Thus, the answer to the question, do demons and fallen angels perform acts of power? The answer is still yes. Jesus said that the enemy has "power" that "hurt," except their powers cannot hurt Jesus or Jesus' disciples.

Ephesians 1:20-21, NIV: [20]*... He raised him from the dead and seated him at his right hand in the **heavenly realms**, [21]**far above** all rule and authority, **power** and dominion, and every title that can be given, not only in the present age but also in the one to come.*

There are indeed "powers" in the heavenly realms. Some of these powers of heaven are between the "far" heavenly realm (third heavens) and the heaven on earth. However, remember that Jesus is "far above" these powers; and they are "subjected" to Jesus **(1 Peter 3:22)**. Thus Jesus, at His will, can convey us pass these powers into the third heaven **(2 Corinthians 12:1-4)**. With that said, let us now look at some of the examples of miracles, sings and power acts that are satanic in nature.

Revelation 16:13-14: [13]*And I saw **three unclean spirits** like frogs coming out of the mouth of the dragon, out of the mouth of the beast, and out of the mouth of the false prophet.* [14]*For **they are spirits of demons, performing signs**, which go out to the kings of the earth and of the whole world, to gather them to the battle of that great day of God Almighty.*

In the text above, the dragon (a spirit), the beast (a spirit, a system, and a person), and the false prophet (symbolic of a spirit, a man, and a group of false prophets) all had unclean spirits come out of their mouths that performed signs. The purpose of these pseudo signs is to deceive the kings of the habitable world to enter the battle of that great day of God Almighty. Thus, these signs are done to deceive, presidents, prime ministers, kings of tribes, kings of nations, princes, queens, leaders, etc.

Exodus 7:9-12: [9]*"When Pharaoh speaks to you, saying, 'Show **a miracle** for yourselves,' then you shall say to Aaron, 'Take your **rod** and cast it before Pharaoh, **and let it become a serpent.**'"* [10]*... And Aaron cast down his rod before Pharaoh and before his servants, and it became a serpent.* [11]***But Pharaoh also called the wise men and the sorcerers; so, the magicians of Egypt, they also did in like manner*** *with their enchantments.* ¹²*For every man threw down his rod, and they became serpents.* **But Aaron's rod swallowed up their rods.**

We see above that God called the act of Moses' rod being turned into a serpent a **"miracle."** When Moses and Aaron performed this miracle, the wise men and sorcerers of Egypt did a similar miracle. Thus, there is no doubt that miracles can be performed illegally. The only difference is that the magician of Egypt was limited in their powers relative to the finger of God.

Exodus 7:20-22: ²⁰*And Moses and Aaron ... lifted up the rod and struck the waters that were in the river .... And all the waters that were in the* ***river were turned to blood*** *....* ²²*Then the magicians of Egypt* ***did so*** *with their enchantments....*

Exodus 8:6-7: ⁶*So Aaron stretched out his hand over the waters of Egypt, and the* ***frogs came up*** *and covered the land of Egypt.* ⁷*And the magicians* ***did so*** *with their enchantments and brought up frogs on the land of Egypt.*

Exodus 8:17-19: ¹⁷*... Aaron stretched out his hand with his rod and struck the dust of the earth, and it became lice on man and beast ....* ¹⁸*Now the magicians so worked with their enchantments to bring forth lice,* ***but they could not*** *....* ¹⁹*Then the magicians said to Pharaoh,* **"This is the finger of God"** *....*

In the texts we just read, we see that Moses and Aaron performed three miracles/signs that the sorcerers of Egypt were able to copy. However, they were limited in their powers. The sorcerers (Jannes and Jambres) were able to miraculously turn their rod into "dragons" like Aaron had done with his rod. However, Aaron's rod swallowed their rods. The sorcerers were able to miraculously turn the waters into blood like Moses and Aaron did. Yet, the sorcerers could not change blood back into water.

The sorcerers were able to multiply frogs, like the three beasts did in Revelation 16:13-14; however, they could not get rid of the frogs (unclean spirits). Finally, God showed Jannes' and Jambres' limited powers when they could not make "lice" miraculously appear. These workers of lawlessness had to finally acknowledge that the miracles demonstrated by Moses and Aaron were done by "the finger of God."

With that said, even though the sorcerers were limited in miraculous powers, they were able to mimic three (3) of Moses and Aaron's miracles. A magician in Acts 8 also caused the people of Samaria to believe he was a "great power of God."

Acts 8:9-10: ⁹But there was a certain man called Simon, who previously practiced sorcery in the city and astonished the people of Samaria, claiming that he was someone great, ¹⁰to whom they all gave heed, from the least to the greatest, saying, **"This man is the great power of God."**

Yes, it is possible for spirits and men/women who are given over to sorcery and "the lie" to produce false miracles (powers). False miracles will also be produced in the last days by those who believe/practice "the lie" in any of its facets. The deception of "the lie" will be believed by the deceived through the energy of error (or seduction) supplied by the energy of Satan as Satan shows all power of falsehood, signs of falsehood and wonders of falsehood.

2 Thessalonians 2:3-11: ³Let no one deceive you by any means; for that Day will not come unless the falling away comes first, and the man of sin is revealed, the son of perdition, ⁴who opposes and exalts himself above all that is called God or that is worshiped, so that he sits as God in the temple of God, **showing** *himself that he is God …. ⁷For the mystery of lawlessness is already at work …. ⁸And then the lawless one will be revealed, whom the Lord will consume with the breath of His mouth and destroy with the brightness of His coming. ⁹The coming of [the lawless one] is according to the* **working of Satan (lit., energy of Satan), with all power, signs, and lying wonders,** *¹⁰… because they did not receive the love of the truth, that they might be saved. ¹¹And for this reason God will send them* **strong delusion (lit., energy of error (or seduction, deception))**, *that they should believe* **the lie.**

I expect that the verses above may seem a little easier to grasp now, relative to false miraculous power. "The man of sin, the son of perdition" will be **"showing** himself that he is god." We learned in a previous chapter, that "showing" is also associated with miracles, wonders, etc. "Jesus of Nazareth, a Man **attested (or showing)** by God to you **by miracles, wonders, and signs** … **(Acts 2:22).**

Paul also indicated that the man of sin, the "lawless one" will be revealed (uncovered) through satanic energy that produces false powers, false signs, and false wonder. The energy of Satan, or energy of error (lit., deception) is what Paul says is the catalyst into believing "the lie." False miracles exist today as it did in the days of Moses, Jesus, Paul, etc. The apostle Paul said, "Now as Jannes and Jambres resisted Moses, so do these also resist **the truth**.…" **(2 Timothy 3:8).** The false prophet, alias, another beast will also deceive by great signs—fire out of heaven—just as Satan did in the book of Job.

Revelation 13:11; 13: [11]*Then I saw **another beast** coming up out of the earth, and he had two horns like a lamb and spoke like a dragon …* [13]*He performs **great signs**, so that he even makes **fire** come down from heaven on the earth in the sight of men.*

Job 1:12; 16: [12]*And the LORD said to **Satan**, "Behold, all that he has is in **your power** ….* [16]*While he was still speaking, another also came and said, "**The fire** of God **fell from heaven** and burned up the sheep and the servants and consumed them.…*

A messenger in the book of Job and some of mankind in Revelation 13 mistakenly thought the "fire" from heaven was "of God." However, the fire was from the "power (hand)" of the **"fiery** dragon," Satan and "another beast." There are pseudo miracles produced from the lie. Jesus himself said that some who claim to be the subjects of Jesus will be rejected, because He never knew them by seeing them. They will be rejected; because they were working lawlessness, even though what appeared to be miracles were associated with their lives

Matthew 7:21-23: [21]*"Not everyone who says to Me, 'Lord, Lord,' shall enter the kingdom of heaven, but he who does the will of My Father in*

heaven. ²²"Many will say to Me in that day, 'Lord, Lord, have we not prophesied in Your name, cast out demons in Your name, and done many wonders in Your name?' ²³"And then I will declare to them, 'I never knew you; depart from Me, you who practice lawlessness!'"

Jesus' Covenant — the Remedy for Lawlessness

Hebrews 10:16-17: *[16]"This is **the covenant** that I will make with them after those days, says the LORD: I will put My laws into their hearts, and in their minds I will write them," [17]then He adds, "Their sins and their **lawless deeds I will remember no more**." [18]Now where there is **remission (lit., forgiveness)** of these, there is no longer an offering for sin.*

God has ratified a New Covenant through the death and resurrection of Jesus Christ. Through this New Covenant, "the blood of the everlasting covenant," the Father has "forgiven" us and justified us. If we repent (change the mind), and if we ask for forgiveness, through the offering of Jesus Christ, our sins, and lawless deeds He will **"no more"** remember. This is good news!

Hebrews 13:20-21: *[20]Now may the God of peace who brought up our Lord Jesus from the dead, that great Shepherd of the sheep, through **the blood of the everlasting covenant**, [21]make you **complete** in every good work to do His will, working in you what is well pleasing in His sight, through Jesus Christ, to whom be glory forever and ever. Amen.*

If mankind will receive the "blood of the everlasting covenant" that Jesus is our atonement and mercy, then all of the practices of lawlessness will be covered under His blood and forgotten. One of the reasons why some cannot receive the love of the truth is that some believe they are unforgivable. Yet, Jesus believed otherwise. Jesus believed that all of our sins can be forgiven, except one sin. All we have to do is receive the love of the truth that Jesus laid down His life for us and believe that He is our atonement.

*Matthew 12:31, KJV: Therefore, I say to you, **every sin** and blasphemy **will be forgiven** men, but the blasphemy against the Spirit will not be forgiven men.*

Matthew 12:31, KJV: Wherefore I say unto you, **all manner of sin** *and* **blasphemy shall be forgiven** *unto men: but the blasphemy against the Holy Ghost shall not be forgiven unto men.*

Jesus not only said that "every sin" is forgivable; but He also said that "all **manner** of sin." is forgivable.[13] This to me heals those who think that the **"manner"** in which they have sinned are unforgivable. According to Jesus all **"manner"** of sin shall be forgiven. Again, "all manner of sin" or "every sin" can be forgiven, except for blasphemy against the Holy Spirit.

All we have to do is ask the Father for forgiveness through "the blood of the everlasting covenant;" and He will forgive us. "If we confess our sins, **He is faithful** and **just** to forgive us our sins and to cleanse us from all unrighteousness" **(1 John 1:9)**. The Lord is full of compassion, and He will abundantly pardon. And there is more! The Lord does not remember our sins; and He does not bring up our former lawlessness. He will not even be reminded of our lawlessness in the future once we receive His forgiveness. The Lord is a covenant God. Covenant says, "Once I have forgiven you, I do not bring it up again." Covenant says, The Father will not allow you to fail once you accept His covenant.

So, I encourage you, turn from all that the lie encompasses to serve the living God. Enter His everlasting covenant, ratified by the blood of Jesus Christ. The Father is not like us humans. He is loving and willing to forgive us of sins and lawlessness if we "receive" His love—"the love of the truth." He is in covenant with Jesus and with us if we receive the sacrifice of Jesus and His atonement for our sins and lawlessness.

Remember the only reason He turned some over to believe "the lie" and to eventually "work lawlessness" is "because they received not the love of the truth, that they might be saved" **(2 Thessalonians 2:10b)**. The blood covenant of Jesus is the remedy for lawlessness. *"And according to the law almost all things are*

---

[13] See my book ***Forgiven 490 Times.***

*purified with blood, and **without shedding of blood** there is no remission"* **(Hebrews 9:22b).** We overcome by the blood of the Lamb. **(Revelation 12:11).**

"Blessed be the glory of the Lord from His Place!"

By Donald Peart, called to be a son of God

Other Books

Poiema, by Judith Peart
Wisdom from Above, by Judith Peart
Procreation, Understanding Sex, and Identity, by Judith Peart
100 Nevers, by Judith Peart
The Shattered and the Healing by Judith Peart
The Lamb, by Donald Peart
Jesus' Resurrection, Our Inheritance, by Donald Peart.
Sexuality, By Donald Peart
Forgiven 490, by Donald Peart w/Judith Peart!
The Days of the Seventh Angel, By Donald Peart
The Torah (The Principle) of Giving, by Donald Peart
The Time Came, by Donald Peart
The Last Hour, the First Hour, the Forty-Second Generation, by Donald Peart
Vision Real, by Donald Peart
The False Prophet, Alias, Another Beast V1, by Donald Peart
"the beast," by Donald Peart
Son of Man Prophesy Against the false prophet, by Donald Peart
The Dragon's Tail, the Prophets who Teach Lies, by Donald Peart
The Work of Lawlessness Revealed, by Donald Peart
When the Lord Made the Tempter, by Donald Peart
Examining Doctrine, Volume 1, by Donald Peart
Exousia, Your God Given Authority, by Donald Peart
The Numbers of God, by Donald Peart
The Completions of the Ages ... by Donald Peart
The Revelation of Jesus Christ, by Donald Peart
Jude—Translation and Commentary, by Donald Peart
Obtaining the Better Resurrection, by Donald Peart
Manifestations from Our Lord Jesus ...by Donald and Judith Peart).
Obtaining the Better Resurrection, by Donald Peart
The New Testament, Dr. Donald Peart Exegesis
The Tree of Life, By Dr. Donald Peart
The Spirit and Power of John, the Baptist by Dr. Donald Peart
The Shattered and the Healing by Judith Peart
Is She Married to a Husband? by Donald Peart
The Ugliest Man God Made by Donald Peart
Does Answering the Call of God Impact Your Children? by Donald Peart
Victory Out-of-the Beast-the Harvest of the Earth by Donald Peart
The Order of Melchizedek by Donald Peart
Ezekiel-the House-the City-the Land (Interpreting the Patterns), by Donald Peart
Butter and Honey, Understanding how to Choose the Good and Refuse Evil, by Donald Peart

Contact Information:
Crown of Glory Ministries
P.O. Box 1041 Randallstown, MD 21133
donaldpeart7@gmail.com

ABOUT THE AUTHOR

Donald Peart is married to Judith Peart. Donald committed his life (though for a short period) while Judith recommitted her life to the Lord Jesus around the summer of 1981 after the pair kept reading the book of John and the book of Revelation. Donald read the entire book of Revelation and became especially interested in Revelation 20:4. Eventually, in April 1986, Donald and Judith permanently recommitted their lives to the Lord Jesus. They have been serving the Lord Jesus since and declaring the well-message of Jesus, the Christ. Over the years, the Lord Jesus has worked various manifestations of signs, wonders, and miracles through them. Below are three examples of the Lord Jesus' involvement in the lives of Donald and Judith.

In 1988, while living in North Carolina, the voice of the Lord spoke to Donald and said, "I have not called you to be an apostle, pastor, evangelist, teacher, but a ...(Donald blocked out the rest of the words the Lord was speaking to Him; because at the time, Donald was afraid God would call him to function in a ministry contrary to what Donald believed he should be functioning as--a prophet)." Approximately seventeen years later, on February 6, 2005, in Maryland, while Donald was on a fast; on the 13th day of the fast, the Lord Jesus resumed the conversation he had with Donald in 1988. As Donald listened, the voice of the Lord continued exactly as He spoke in 1988, "I have not called you to be a prophet, an apostle, an evangelist, a pastor, or teacher, but I have called you to be a son."

In 1990, while in prayer speaking to the heavenly Father about going to university to study engineering, Donald heard the Lord Jesus say to him "you are as Joseph before me; go to engineering school; you will be good at it." The Lord also said to Donald, "this is the sign that I have spoken to you; your wife is pregnant with a girl." Donald responded to the Lord saying, "Joseph did not have any daughters." To which the Lord replied, "Joseph is a fruitful son, a fruitful son by a well whose daughters run over the wall." Donald immediately searched the Scriptures to see if Joseph had any daughters. The Scriptures confirmed that what the Lord spoke to Donald was correct. Genesis 49:22, translated from the Hebrew, states "Joseph is a fruitful son, a fruitful son by a well whose daughters run over the wall." The "sign" the Lord gave to Donald was fulfilled immediately. Judith Peart was already pregnant with their third child; a girl named Charity was born to them according to the time of life. Donald also graduated from engineering school. In addition to their five natural children, they have spiritual "daughters" and "sons " because God is fulfilling His word to them. This was also the second and third time the Lord called Donald a son.

On a day around 1991, Donald became disheartened, and he spoke to the Lord about his circumstances. At the time, he and his wife were experiencing extreme trials after Donald's obedience to the Lord. Donald was instructed to study God's Word exclusively, which turned out to be almost four years of intense study and prayer coupled with a time of consistent acute trials or probe-testing. As Donald sat on the sofa that day reading Genesis 2, the Lord began unveiling to Donald an understanding of Genesis 2 with an understanding he had not heard the elders teach. The Spirit of the Lord began to show Donald the sequence of creation, including the man (Adam), the original serpent, and Mrs. Adam (later called Eve). As the Spirit of Jesus revealed to Donald how the Scriptures in Genesis 2 should be interpreted, his mind began questioning what he was reading and hearing in the Spirit. His mind questioned the revelation of the Holy Spirit due to previous doctrines he learned in church from the elders and commentaries. As Donald questioned the understanding the Spirit of God revealed to him, Donald saw the pages of the Bible he was reading being closed one by one, yet the physical Bible in his lap was still opened to the same pages he was reading. This is when he realized he was seeing a vision. The Lord then said to him, "Do not filter My Word through what the elders have taught you."

As a result of the Lord making Himself know to Donald and Judith throughout the years and providing explicit directions to Donald with regards God's doctrine, Donald and Judith have preached the gospel of Christ as the Lord has taught him; a gospel that is centered on Jesus Christ, the Son of the living God and the bride of Christ. With that said, the Lord Jesus has also graced Donald Peart to earn diplomas from Baltimore Polytechnic High School; an Associate of Arts degree in Pre-Engineering, a Bachelor of Science degree in Civil Engineering, a Master of Divinity, a Master of Science in Construction Management, and a Doctorate in Theology.

www.ingramcontent.com/pod-product-compliance
Lightning Source LLC
Chambersburg PA
CBHW032214040426
42449CB00005B/586